Sisters
A Daily Journal of Memories

Created by:

Joanne Barber Farrell
and
Kathleen Barber Lashier

Copyright © 1998, Shoestrings

ShoeStrings

P.O. Box 31
Pelican Lake, WI 54463
1-800-554-1345
Fax: 715-487-5529

Printed in the U.S.A.
G & R Publishing Co.

Distributed By:

507 Industrial Street
Waverly, IA 50677
Phone: 800-887-4445
Fax: 800-886-7496

ISBN #1-56383-071-X

ITEM #5050

Joanne & Kathy

Joanne and Kathy's childhood memories center around their early years in Iowa.

Joanne and her husband Dave have two grown sons, Mark and Greg, and now live in northern Wisconsin.

Kathy and her husband Jack, also the parents of two grown sons, Andrew and Jackson, have remained in Iowa.

Every summer "at the lake" in Wisconsin, the growing family continues to create precious memories, mostly involving food, campfires, games, water sports, star-gazing, story telling, and laughter.

*With loving appreciation for the memories
that they helped to create,
we dedicate this book to our parents,
John and Virginia Barber,
and to our brother, David.*

*We would like to thank all of our friends and relatives
who contributed photos for this book.*

Memory Journals for Special People

TO:

FROM:

Place photo of you & your sister here

*When we were young, we sometimes
celebrated the New Year by . . .*

January 1

One of my earliest memories of you is . . .

January 2

The names of our family members and their dates and places of birth are . . .

January 3

This is where each of us lives now.

January 4

Mom or Dad always said you were . . .

January 5

Remember the time when I helped you . . .

January 6

Movies that were popular when I was in high school were . . .

January 7

An imaginary friend I had was . . .

January 8

Mom and Dad always tell me about
when I used to say… "

January 9

I remember that you collected . . .

January 10

And I collected . . .

January 11

One of your birthdays that I especially remember is . . .

January 12

One of my birthdays that I remember is . . .

January 13

You add so much to our family.

January 14

The pets I remember most are . . .

January 15

A good pet story from our childhood was when . . .

January 16

A nickname we had for you was

because . . .

January 17

A nickname you had for me was

because . . .

January 18

When we were sick, Mom/Dad always . . .

January 19

A winter storm I remember is . . .

January 20

A memory I have of going sliding is . . .

January 21

I remember playing in the snow.

January 22

A big difference between us was . . .

January 23

I wish we could see each other more often
so we could . . .

January 24

I love my nieces/nephews because . . .

January 25

After we were supposed to be asleep,
we . . .

January 26

Songs that were popular when I was in high school were . . .

January 27

Remember when we ice skated?

January 28

People probably thought we were crazy when . . .

January 29

I always think of you when I see . . .

January 30

I remember putting on performances for our parents.

January 31

When we had to do the dishes, we always . . .

February 1

A time when we tried to cook alone was . . .

February 2

We were so scared when . . .

February 3

A time when you made me feel safer was . . .

February 4

You used to drive me crazy when you . . .

February 5

A memory I have of your wedding is . . .

February 6

Some of our family sayings were . . .

February 7

A story Daddy always told us was . . .

February 8

After I was grown, when I went back home I always . . .

February 9

A card game we liked to play was . . .

February 10

You always beat me at . . .

February 11

The things I remember most about long winter evenings are . . .

February 12

A Valentine I made was . . .

February 13

A special Valentine surprise from Mom or Dad was . . .

February 14

A trip I'd like to take you on is . . .

February 15

School activities I remember from high school are . . .

February 16

I remember activities that you were in too.

February 17

A time when I felt really grown up was . . .

February 18

Some of your elementary school friends I remember are . . .

February 19

Some of my elementary school friends I remember are . . .

February 20

I remember an old car we had.

February 21

A new car we got was . . .

February 22

We had a flat tire when . . .

February 23

Books I loved in high school were . . .

February 24

We used to pretend that . . .

February 25

A favorite board game we used to play was . . .

February 26

Some of my pet peeves are . . .

February 27

A few of my favorite things are . . .

February 28

Once we tricked Mom or Dad by...

March 1

A scent I remember from Grandma's house is . . .

March 2

How technology has changed!
In elementary school we listened to music
on the . . .

March 3

Later we listened to popular songs on . . .

March 4

A special church ceremony I remember was . . .

March 5

When we got mad at each other, we sometimes . . .

March 6

A favorite winter treat that Mom or Dad
made was . . .

March 7

A food that I wish I could make as good as Mom's is . . .

March 8

These are some stories I've been told about my birth.

March 9

These are stories I've been told (or remember) about your birth.

March 10

I remember Mom telling stories about when she was young.

March 11

I remember Dad telling stories about when he was young.

March 12

When I was in high school, a feature of my appearance that I wanted to change was . . .

March 13

On weekends we often . . .

March 14

My favorite time of year is _____,
because . . .

March 15

My least favorite time of year is
_____, *because . . .*

March 16

Something I remember about St. Patrick's Day is . . .

March 17

A scent that always reminds me of our home is . . .

March 18

A time we got to go someplace alone was . . .

March 19

*A terrible snowstorm we traveled
in was . . .*

March 20

I remember going to the doctor when we were young.

A memory I have of going to church when we were growing up is . . .

March 22

A time when we flew kites was . . .

March 23

We could always tell spring was coming because . . .

March 24

(If the following Easter topics do not apply, please share your special Holiday memories and traditions.)

I remember our Easter Egg Hunts.

March 25

A special Easter church service that I remember is . . .

March 26

Some Easter traditions our family had were . . .

March 27

We played for hours on the swing set . . .

March 28

If I could return to my childhood,
something I would do differently is...

March 29

If I were a teenager again, I would . . .

March 30

The biggest physical problem I've had to deal with is . . .

March 31

An April Fool's Day joke I remember is . . .

April 1

When we were young, you often tried to trick me by . . .

April 2

I remember that we were always afraid of . . .

April 3

Of all your girlfriends and boyfriends, my favorites were_____, because . . .

April 4

My least favorites were_____,
because . . .

April 5

_____taught me how to
drive a car in our_____
_____.

April 6

*When I first started driving, gas cost
_____, and I paid for it by . . .*

April 7

I don't think Mom or Dad ever found out about when we . . .

April 8

I remember some of the baby-sitters we had.

April 9

Some baby-sitter memories that stand out are . . .

April 10

When I was in high school, dances that were popular were . . .

April 11

The first dances I went to were . . .

April 12

A high school prom I remember is . . .

April 13

A war I remember is . . .

April 14

This is what I remember most about that time.

April 15

In my early memories of you, you looked like this.

April 16

. . .And I looked like this.

April 17

One of my birthday cakes that I remember is . . .

April 18

One of your birthday cakes I remember is . . .

April 19

When you were _____, you always got into trouble by . . .

April 20

Some rules at our house were . . .

April 21

You made me laugh when . . .

April 22

One of our saddest moments was . . .

April 23

You were always better than I was at . . .

April 24

I was always better than you at . . .

April 25

A dangerous thing we did when we were little was . . .

April 26

The bravest thing we ever did was . . .

April 27

I think my favorite thing I owned was my . . .

April 28

My favorite thing you owned was your . . .

April 29

Remember when the greatest new invention was . . .

April 30

We made May Baskets . . .

May 1

A relative we always loved to visit was
_____,
because . . .

May 2

A relative we did not like to visit was
_____,

because . . .

May 3

I remember when we hid_____
_____from Mom or Dad.
When they found it, they . . .

May 4

When I was little, I wanted to be a
_____ *when I grew up*
because . . .

May 5

I think my best talent now is . . .

May 6

I think your best talent now is . . .

May 7

We are most alike in the following ways.

May 8

We are most different in the following ways.

May 9

A funny childhood memory of our brother/ sister is . . .

May 10

A high school memory of our brother/sister is . . .

May 11

When we were little, I always thought
Mom or Dad liked you better when . . .

May 12

A special memory I have of our Grandma is . . .

May 13

Mom was really good at making . . .

May 14

One of my favorite memories about our Mom is . . .

May 15

When I think about Mom, I always picture her . . .

May 16

Some advice Mom always gave me was . . .

May 17

Spring reminds me of the flowers we had.

May 18

A spring chore I always dreaded was . . .

May 19

Special activities I remember from my senior year are . . .

May 20

Special activities I remember from your senior year are . . .

May 21

The year and place of my high school graduation were . . .

May 22

The parts of my high school building that I remember the most are . . .

May 23

Some special people I remember from high school are . . .

May 24

I could hardly wait to get out of high school so I could . . .

May 25

On Memorial Day we always . . .

May 26

A parade memory I have is . . .

May 27

A "last-day-of-school" I especially remember is . . .

May 28

We were excited about summer so we could . . .

May 29

I remember going fishing.

May 30

*My favorite high school hairstyle
looked like this.*

May 31

Remember staying at Grandma's house?

June 1

One of my favorite things that Grandma had in her house was . . .

June 2

When I think of playing dolls with you, I remember . . .

June 3

Another favorite doll play memory is . . .

June 4

The best things about growing up in our family were . . .

June 5

Sometimes I thought the <u>worst</u> thing about growing up in our family was . . .

June 6

A high school "hang-out" in our town was
_____,
and this is what we usually did there.

June 7

Remember playing hide and seek?

June 8

A favorite hiding place we had was . . .

June 9

I remember being at the swimming pool . . .

June 10

Some places we went to on summer trips were . . .

June 11

An exciting part of one of our trips was . . .

June 12

A funny part of one of our trips was . . .

June 13

A good story I remember about Dad is . . .

June 14

When I think about Dad I always picture him . . .

June 15

Some advice Dad always gave us was . . .

June 16

Dad was always good at making . . .

June 17

A special memory I have of our Grandpa is . . .

June 18

I always think of you when I hear the song, . . .

June 19

At home we always had to help . . .

June 20

Remember the bicycles we had?

June 21

This is what I remember about you and me learning to ride bikes.

June 22

A favorite place we rode on our bikes was . . .

June 23

This is what I remember about you and me getting hurt on our bikes.

June 24

A memory I have of summer camp is . . .

June 25

I remember a picnic we went on.

June 26

A memory I have of our brother/sister as an adult is . . .

June 27

The biggest mess we ever made together was . . .

June 28

Our favorite part of car trips was . .

June 29

Some food we often took on trips with us . . .

June 30

When we rode in the car, we always fought about . . .

July 1

A time when we got lost on a trip was . . .

July 2

When we were little, we often watched
fireworks at . . .

July 3

A 4ᵗʰ of July tradition we had when we were older was . . .

July 4

*I remember a time when I was down
and you were there for me.*

July 5

A big change in our lives came when . . .

July 6

My first airplane ride was . . .

July 7

An outside chore we always had in the summer was . . .

July 8

The things I remember most about long summer evenings are . . .

July 9

I remember a surprise birthday party.

July 10

I've probably annoyed you when I . . .

July 11

When my friends were over, you often . . .

July 12

When your friends were around, I liked to …

July 13

A memory I have of swimming in a lake or ocean is . . .

July 14

You and your friends were mean to me when . . .

July 15

You and your friends were nice to me when . . .

July 16

An outside game we made up was
_____*, and the*
rules were . . .

July 17

My favorite nature places have been . . .

July 18

The tree house or fort we had (or always wanted to have) was . . .

July 19

I could hardly wait to get my driver's license so I could . . .

July 20

I can remember pretending that . . .

July 21

We cooled off in the summer by . . .

July 22

A craft, building, or creative project I remember working on was . . .

July 23

I remember when we went camping . . .

July 24

When we were kids we usually earned money by . . .

July 25

The worst scheme either of us ever had for earning money was . . .

July 26

The celebrity I am most like would probably be . . .

July 27

The celebrity that you are most like would probably be . . .

July 28

Something I borrowed from you was . . .

July 29

Something you borrowed from me was . . .

July 30

When I wanted to go some place, I could usually talk _____ into letting me go by . . .

I remember a time when I got home really late.

August 1

Our poor pets! Remember when we . . .

August 2

An early experience with make-up was . . .

August 3

A gift you gave me that I love is . . .

August 4

I first tried smoking when . . .

August 5

My "career plan" when I graduated from high school was . . .

August 6

I think a perfect career for you would be . . .

August 7

I especially remember Aunt _____
when she . . .

August 8

I especially remember Uncle
_____ *when he . . .*

August 9

I liked going to Aunt _____'s house because . . .

August 10

A favorite summer treat that Mom or Dad made was . . .

August 11

Remember when we went to the park and . . .

August 12

When I was a child, I worried about . . .

August 13

The chore we always disliked the most was . . .

August 14

I remember when you left home . . .

August 15

I remember when I left home . . .

August 16

I remember my first car . . .

August 17

I remember your first car . . .

August 18

A secret club we had was . . .

August 19

When we were little, we loved to watch
_____ *on TV.*

August 20

*When we were in jr. high and high school,
our favorite TV shows were . . .*

August 21

One of the earliest days of school that I clearly recall was…

August 22

I could hardly wait to be in high school so I could . . .

August 23

In elementary school I got back and forth by . . .

August 24

In jr. high school I got to school by . . .

August 25

When I was in high school, I got there by . . .

August 26

Instead of behaving in class,
sometimes my friends and I . . .

August 27

A time I got into trouble in school was . . .

August 28

I can remember getting ready to start a new school year by . . .

August 29

The elementary teachers I remember are . . .

August 30

One of my favorite teachers was . . .

August 31

When you were in elementary school,
I remember you . . .

September 1

When you were in high school, I remember you . . .

September 2

Getting up to get ready for school was always . . .

September 3

Some new school clothes I remember were . . .

September 4

Remember when Mom or Dad used to make us wear . . .

September 5

Some hand-me-down clothes we shared were . . .

September 6

I remember a time when I got spanked.

September 7

I remember a time when you got spanked.

September 8

When we had to study . . .

September 9

During elementary school, my favorite books were . . .

September 10

I can remember when Mom or Dad read to us from . . .

September 11

The scent of autumn leaves always reminds me of . . .

September 12

On the first day of school, I always felt . . .

September 13

A teacher everybody always wanted in high school was . . .

September 14

A teacher we all dreaded getting was . . .

September 15

Teachers probably dreaded getting my friends and me because . . .

September 16

Teachers probably dreaded getting your friends and you because . . .

September 17

When we were in elementary school, this is what we usually wore.

September 18

A typical high school outfit was . . .

September 19

I thought the smartest kid in my class was _____ because . . .

September 20

During recess my friends and I liked to . . .

September 21

When I was young I tried to imitate . . .

September 22

I remember a time when we were thinking about the same thing.

September 23

I have felt closest to you when . . .

September 24

When I think of all you've done,
I am most proud of you for . . .

September 25

*Shopping together with you is_____,
because . . .*

September 26

Mom always used to tell us . . .

September 27

I wish I were more like you . . .

September 28

If we could own a business together, we should . . .

September 29

We used to look forward to winter so we could . . .

September 30

An inside game we made up was
_____*, and the*
rules were . . .

October 1

Songs we used to sing were . . .

October 2

We fought about . . .

October 3

We laughed about . . .

October 4

I remember the bedrooms we had.

October 5

Sharing a room with you was . . .

October 6

The first house I remember living in was . . .

October 7

Other houses I remember are . . .

October 8

When we took baths, we liked to . . .

October 9

A house we always like to visit was . . .

October 10

If we could trade lives for a day, I think I would most enjoy . . .

October 11

I think I would least enjoy . . .

October 12

A famous person who died when we were young was . . .

October 13

I remember a time when the electricity went out.

October 14

Because you were (older, younger), you always got to . . .

October 15

I think of you when I eat . . .

October 16

I remember raking leaves.

October 17

A game we played in the leaves was . . .

October 18

A movie Mom or Dad thought was too grown-up for me to see was . . .

October 19

A performer or band that adults thought was indecent was . . .

October 20

While growing up, my favorite meal was . . .

October 21

My least favorite meal was . . .

October 22

When we didn't want to eat what was on our plates, . . .

October 23

At the dinner table we usually . . .

October 24

I remember spending time with these cousins . . .

October 25

Among my most memorable cousin adventures are . . .

October 26

Your kids are so much like you when they . . .

October 27

The ghost story we always liked to hear was . . .

October 28

The time when I was most afraid of a ghost or "monster" was . . .

October 29

Some Halloween costumes I especially remember are . . .

October 30

A favorite trick-or-treat memory was . . .

October 31

A time when we surprised Mom
& Dad was…

November 1

What I remember most about fall football games was . . .

November 2

This is what I remember most about Homecoming.

November 3

Some early presidential elections I remember are . . .

November 4

The first time I ever voted for president
was in _____.

I voted for _____
because . . .

November 5

One of my favorite times spent with you is . . .

November 6

Here is something I would like to say to you but never have.

November 7

This is a poem I wrote especially for you.

November 8

These are the neighbor kids I remember.

November 9

Some of our memorable neighborhood moments include . . .

November 10

Mom and Dad never agreed with me about . . .

November 11

An early memory I have of something BIG in the news is . . .

November 12

Some family friends I remember are . . .

November 13

When they visited our house, we usually . . .

November 14

When we went to visit _____,
we usually . . .

November 15

We were anxious for snow so we could . . .

November 16

*When we were in high school, something
we thought was really shocking was . . .*

November 17

We always used to say/sing this rhyme.

November 18

The craziest song lyrics I remember from our early years are . . .

November 19

When I was young, I was thankful for our family when . . .

November 20

Now I am thankful for . . .

November 21

On Thanksgiving we usually . . .

November 22

Our favorite Thanksgiving foods were . . .

November 23

I remember when school was cancelled because . . .

November 24

In high school we weren't supposed to wear . . .

November 25

A family cure for injuries was . . .

November 26

An embarrassing moment I remember is . . .

November 27

I remember when you and your high school friends . . .

November 28

When I was in high school, some of my favorite singers were . . .

November 29

(If the following Christmas topics do not apply, please share your special Holiday memories and traditions.)

Mom or Dad always made Christmas special by…

November 30

My favorite Christmas cookies were . . .

December 1

We decorated the outside of our house by . . .

December 2

We decorated the inside of our house by . . .

December 3

We went to see Santa Claus at . . .

December 4

My earliest ideas about Santa were . . .

December 5

Something I really wanted for Christmas was . . .

December 6

A present we waited a long time for was . . .

December 7

I remember being in church programs.

December 8

We usually got our Christmas trees at . . .

December 9

A funny Christmas tree incident I remember is . . .

December 10

The ornaments I treasured most were . . .

December 11

When we decorated the tree, we always . . .

December 12

A special gift or surprise we had for Mom was . . .

December 13

A special gift or surprise we had for Dad was . . .

December 14

I remember snooping for presents.

December 15

The first year we were apart for Christmas was . . .

December 16

I remember when Santa brought us . . .

December 17

Something I always remember about
Christmas at Grandma's house is . . .

December 18

A special present I made was . . .

December 19

I remember when you gave me a . . .

December 20

I'll always remember . . .

December 21

During Christmas vacation we loved to . . .

December 22

We always got ready for Santa by . . .

December 23

A Christmas Eve tradition we had was . . .

December 24

On Christmas Day . . .

December 25

A trip we took during Christmas vacation was . . .

December 26

A special wish I have for you is . . .

December 27

Something I did this year that I am proud of is . . .

December 28

Something that was really hard for me this year was . . .

December 29

The best time we had together this year was . . .

December 30

And in closing –

December 31

More thoughts, stories, memories . . .

More thoughts, stories, memories . . .

More thoughts, stories, memories . . .

More thoughts, stories, memories . . .

More thoughts, stories, memories . . .